CW00346954

1,000,000 Books

are available to read at

———◆———

www.ForgottenBooks.com

———◆———

Read online
Download PDF
Purchase in print

ISBN 978-1-331-67702-4
PIBN 10220152

This book is a reproduction of an important historical work. Forgotten Books uses state-of-the-art technology to digitally reconstruct the work, preserving the original format whilst repairing imperfections present in the aged copy. In rare cases, an imperfection in the original, such as a blemish or missing page, may be replicated in our edition. We do, however, repair the vast majority of imperfections successfully; any imperfections that remain are intentionally left to preserve the state of such historical works.

Forgotten Books is a registered trademark of FB &c Ltd.
Copyright © 2018 FB &c Ltd.
FB &c Ltd, Dalton House, 60 Windsor Avenue, London, SW19 2RR.
Company number 08720141. Registered in England and Wales.

For support please visit www.forgottenbooks.com

1 MONTH OF FREE READING

at

www.ForgottenBooks.com

By purchasing this book you are eligible for one month membership to ForgottenBooks.com, giving you unlimited access to our entire collection of over 1,000,000 titles via our web site and mobile apps.

To claim your free month visit:

www.forgottenbooks.com/free220152

* Offer is valid for 45 days from date of purchase. Terms and conditions apply.

English
Français
Deutsche
Italiano
Español
Português

www.forgottenbooks.com

Mythology Photography **Fiction**
Fishing Christianity **Art** Cooking
Essays Buddhism Freemasonry
Medicine **Biology** Music **Ancient**
Egypt Evolution Carpentry Physics
Dance Geology **Mathematics** Fitness
Shakespeare **Folklore** Yoga Marketing
Confidence Immortality Biographies
Poetry **Psychology** Witchcraft
Electronics Chemistry History **Law**
Accounting **Philosophy** Anthropology
Alchemy Drama Quantum Mechanics
Atheism Sexual Health **Ancient History**
Entrepreneurship Languages Sport
Paleontology Needlework Islam
Metaphysics Investment Archaeology
Parenting Statistics Criminology
Motivational

THE PSYCHOLOGICAL ASPECTS OF CHRISTIAN EXPERIENCE

BY

RICHARD H. K. GILL, A.M., Ph.D.

BOSTON

SHERMAN, FRENCH & COMPANY

1915

COPYRIGHT, 1915
SHERMAN, FRENCH & COMPANY

PREFACE

Continued observation of the various methods of religious instruction has brought upon me a conviction that grows stronger as the years go by, that there must be, as Francis Peabody says, a new expansion of the range of studies appropriate to the teachers of religion. There ought to be a far deeper study of the psychology of religion. The appeal to the impulses and emotions, so prevalent in the methods of some teachers, is far behind twentieth century enlightenment. It was foreign to the methods of our Saviour. He taught men. He did not frighten them into action, neither entice them. He instructed their minds in truth. " Ye shall know the truth and the truth shall make you free."

While religious teaching addressed to the head alone may not reach any deeper, the proper inlet by which the truth may reach the soul is the intellect and not the impulses. This brief essay will but sketch some of the mental experiences of religious life, sufficiently, it is hoped, to arouse a desire for further study and deeper investigation of the subject.

CONTENTS

CHAPTER   PAGE

      INTRODUCTION 1

I   SIN 7

II   AWAKENING 20

III   PENITENCE AND REPENTANCE . . . 30

IV   CONVERSION AND REGENERATION . . 36

V   DEVELOPMENT OF CHRISTIAN STRENGTH 45

VI   APOSTASY 58

VII   THE EMOTIONS IN RELIGIOUS LIFE . 68

VIII   CONSCIENCE 85

IX   ILLUSIONS AND HALLUCINATIONS . . 94

CONTENTS

INTRODUCTION

In this study of the psychological aspects of Christian experience, we shall endeavor to follow exclusively the mental states and changes through which the subject passes in the enjoyment of the various phases of Christian experience. We shall not touch the spiritual or doctrinal side at all. Of course these differ with the different sects. But human minds are alike, and pass through similar states and changes in Christian development. More attention ought to be paid to the intellectual side of religion, and less to the sentimental. If Christian ministers would appeal more generally to the intellect and reasoning, and discard that class of preaching that appeals only to the emotions, their work would be more lasting.

As we proceed to examine the psychic changes accompanying the developments of Christian experience, we should not only gain a more intelligent view of what goes on in the mind, but be able to preach the gospel more effectively. If we are to reach the soul through the intellect, we should know just what effect the gospel should have upon it, and what changes of mind

should precede and accompany the development
of character.   By understanding what is going
on in the mind of a person in times of moral
crisis, one ought to be the more able to help him
intelligently.

Many of the statements herein will seem ab-
surd, and even sacrilegious, to those who have
given the subject less study.   In my twelve
years' experience in the ministry, in widely separated communities, and among all classes and
types of people, I have had some opportunity
to give the subject careful study.   While many
of the explanations I shall make will seem to the
uneducated (but as conscientious) believer to
explain away the very sweetness of some of his
most precious experiences, to the student of
psychology they will but add strength to the
doctrines and give additional proof of the genu-
ineness of Christian experience.

The various sects do not lay equal stress upon
all the phases of Christian experience, and all
persons do not experience them alike.   A
Catholic or a Lutheran may look on at a Methodist or Baptist revival with as much curiosity
and as little understanding as if they were
dropped into an entirely new world.   They were
not taught that way.   Indeed, their education
rather prejudices them against such performance.   It is a mystery to them why souls cry
aloud for mercy, why they pray until it con-

vulses the whole body, why they shout for joy when the burden is lifted and they receive the witness of the Spirit, unless we can explain to them the dynamic effect of these experiences upon the mind.

I shall make much of attention. Some may say I have almost idolized it. The deeper I have gone into this study, especially in the close observation of individual subjects, the more thoroughly I am convinced that the greatest problem of religious life, psychologically, is control of the attention. The great task before us is to gain control of the attention and maintain it. If sin never gains attention, it will never get into the life. On the other hand, until righteousness draws the attention of the sinner, there will be no reform. The great task of the revivalist is to keep the people's attention focused upon their sinful condition and its awful consequences until their souls become disgusted with themselves and thoroughly tired of sin. Then when the mercy of Jesus Christ is offered, they are ready to apply any remedy that promises to relieve their morbid minds and souls.

The greatest problem in Christian growth is control of the attention. Keep attention absorbed in the work of God, and do not allow sin or temptation to gain control at all. I remember the title of an old hymn, " Keep your eyes fixed upon Jesus." If by " eyes " we mean attention, there is good theology, and better psychology, in it.

Of course much of our action is not the subject of thought at all, but is controlled by subconsciousness. But what is subconsciousness at any time but the sum of all previous conscious states as they remain in the subliminal self. Nothing will spring from subconsciousness that has not previously been in the active psychic life. But processes started in active psychosis may continue and sometimes be completed in subconsciousness.

It would be an offence to some people to tell them that some of their dearest experiences are illusions, and sometimes entire hallucinations. But facts are stubborn things. We must not allow sentimentality to prevent an intelligent analysis of experience. To me, the scientific explanation of religious facts and experiences only makes them appeal with stronger force. Of course, religion, being spiritual, has more to do with the ego or conscious self that never dies, the breath of divine life breathed into us by our Creator. But this does not forbid the intelligent study of its effects upon the other parts of the self, as it envelops the whole being.

It will be our purpose, in what follows, to study from the standpoint of psychology the mental developments and changes accompanying the various phases of Christian experience, and induced by them, with as impartial view as possible, in order that we may be better able to guide the intellect in healthy moral channels.

CHAPTER I

SIN

Professor Leuba defines the religious sense as " the feeling of unwholeness, of moral imperfection, of sin,— to use the technical word,— together with the yearning after the peace of unity." The word " religion," he says, " is getting more and more to signify the conglomerate of desires and emotions springing from the sense of sin and its release."

The Bible teaches us to believe that we are born in sin and shapen in iniquity, inheriting the sinful nature of our forefathers. We are not responsible for our being born with a sinful nature, nor are we condemned for it. For as in Adam all die, so in Christ, the second Adam, all are made alive again. Then every child of the race is saved by the merits of the atonement until he actually commits wilful sin. Nearly all Christian denominations teach (to use Merrill's words) that " the redemption that secured our probation and our being, secured also the insipient workings of grace in the soul, placing every child of the fallen race in a justified state, in the kingdom of God, and in possession of the germ of life. This is the source of good that is in us all."

The realization of sin and the responsibility for sinful acts will depend greatly upon birth, education and environment. The man born in darkness and reared in ignorance in some heathen country, or in some frontier settlement in our own land, may practise many things contrary to God's law without the least remorse. We need go no further than some of the recesses of our own Alleghanies to find men altogether ignorant of moral law. They live as they were born and raised, without any other motives or impulses save those arising from the appetites and desires of the body. They have known no religion at all. They have no sense of sin because they have no knowledge of the law. They have moved into these regions in search of a livelihood, and in so doing have left behind them all religious and educational influences. In this respect they are more destitute than the heathen tribes of foreign lands, for they have a tribal religion, with its cult, however crude it may be, but these have none at all. We cannot term them in any sense voluntary transgressors of the law. They have little sense of sin, for they have little knowledge of the law.

We find the sense of sin varying with the

teaching of the different denominations. In some liberal churches one may indulge innocently in many things that a Quaker or Methodist would think wrong, and to whom the participation of these things would be sin. For to him that knoweth to do good and doeth it not, to him it is sin. So with those who are not believers, their sense of sin is less acute, especially when what religious education they have is of the more liberal sort.

The sense of sin depends also upon the early training in the home. I have known children born in ungodly homes to be taught to swear. Children have also been taught to steal and fight and cheat, and even made drunk to see them " tight." Now this being done in the early years, before a sense of right and wrong has been developed, although they may be in the midst of the most enlightened Christian community, they will never have much moral sensitiveness until awakened. Had the same child, although born of the most wicked parents and inheriting their wicked natures, been taken from his home and reared in a strict Christian home with strict moral training, while he would develop some of the wicked tendencies born within him, he would yet have a deeper sense of sin. Vice versa,— take a child from the best home during his tender years, and thrust him into a wicked home where he will be taught evil systematically, and he will lose what moral sense he had.

Let us examine the influence of surroundings upon the sense of sin a little more carefully. All animals have the social instinct, and man is the most sociable of them all. There is always a tendency to go with the crowd. A man can be little better than the crowd with which he is intimately associated. There will always be a sort of communal consciousness, a common opinion of the crowd on all issues. " Evil communications corrupt good manners." A man of good birth and training may sink to the level of a ruffian by being associated with ruffians. On the other hand, you may take a man of low birth and no moral training, and place him in the exclusive company of godly men, and his boisterous and sinful habits will be shaded down, and in most cases there will arise within him a sense of admiration for good and a sense of shame for evil.

Now the man born in darkness and living in ignorance, can have no consciousness of sin, for he has no knowledge of the law. Conscience, as we shall see later, is governed by knowledge. But when, after learning the law, he spends a little time in introspection, his attention is drawn to the disagreement of his life and habits with the law. When a man with a moral sense is in the exclusive company of evil, his attention is taken away from good altogether, just as the wicked man's attention is directed to the good by the exclusive company of the godly.

Let us follow the influence of environment a little further, together with evil associations. Some one has said that sin is as contagious as smallpox. In many cases this is true. I know a young physician, who, but for his moral weakness, would be a leader in his profession. If, walking down the street, we should pass a saloon, he would not mention entering unless some of the others did. If I should say, " Come, let us have a drink," he would say, " All right." If, as we were about to enter, I should say, " No; let us go on," he would consent as readily. When for a little while he lived among strict Christian people, he became very religious. But if, while in the home of a patient, he were offered a drink, he could not refuse, although he had no desire for it until offered to him. He would never think of swearing in chaste company, but in a crowd of profane men he could swear as hard as any of them. Of course this is a pathological case. But we can best study many phases of psychic action by the observation of the extreme.

But let us now proceed to examine the man who was born and reared in a Christian home and under normal conditions. Why does he relinquish his primal state of justification and become a sinner? When he knows right from wrong, knows the penalty of sin and the reward of righteousness, why does he sin? Why do his actions thus disagree with what we have a right to believe is his better judgment?

We must admit that there are two diametrically opposing forces at work in the soul. Our first parents were created pure, in the image of God, but with a mind to which sin could appeal. The forbidden fruit looked good. What at first may have been but a morally indifferent judgment, grew into desire as Eve looked at the fruit. Satan said to her, as to all her posterity, " It will do you no harm; you will not die. Eat it if you want it," until Eve's attention was drawn away from the law completely. The desire for the forbidden fruit thus gained the hypertrophy of attention. How often she looked at the fruit before she desired it, and how often she wished for it before the desire, destroying her sense of the law, became strong enough for dynamogenesis, we will never know. But I think in this first sin we have a type of the process by which all sin is committed.

Now not every transgression of God's law is sin. According to the Stoics, sin is a refusal to live according to nature. In the language of Butler, it is a refusal to recognize the voice of conscience. According to Kant, it is declining to obey the categorical imperative. But these are but impersonal names for the sovereignty of God's law. Where there is no enlightenment and no free will, there can be no sin. |SIN IS THE VOLUNTARY TRANSGRESSION OF GOD'S LAW.| Error unconsciously committed through ignorance may help to destroy moral character and cultivate evil appetite, and make right difficult and sin easier, when the mind becomes enlightened, but it is not sin in the true sense.

But why do men voluntarily sin? Not only will education and environment influence them, but the psychic condition at the time of the temptation, and possibly some physical necessity. The man who has been honest all his life, has had no desire for the goods of others, when " dead broke " may become a thief and steal his neighbor's money or produce. The same man may have always been truthful, yet lie about his theft.

Peter had been truthful so far as we know, but when Christ was being tried for his life, and the disciples might also be in danger, he both lied and swore under the pressure of fear. Judas had a weakness for money. I have never thought Judas had any special desire to betray his Lord. But he loved money. He loved the looks of it and the feel of it, just as do many modern men. This greed had shown out before, when he thought the woman wasted the costly oil on the Master. When the Jews offered him the thirty pieces of money, it tempted him at his weakest place. He yielded because of his greed for silver. I believe the money was more inducement to him than any honor they might have offered him.

Much will depend upon the thought occupying the dynamic center immediately before the temptation. Here is a man of the most peaceable type, never known to fight. But he is beset with a number of provocations. Some one has cheated him in a business transaction. Another has cast reproach upon his good name. And he is so angry that he could whip the guilty parties if he could get at them. Here comes one of his best friends, who may say some little thing in mere jest, and he will strike him in the face. Or he may have been at all other times the kindest husband, but if his wife would do the least thing to provoke him while thus irritated, he might scold her violently. If the mind is jubilant at the time, provocation may only bring a smile. Yesterday, while I was exulting over the accomplishment of a certain difficult task, a bit of vile gossip came to me that would have sometimes aroused my indignation and tempted me to say some unpleasant things. But as it was, I just laughed and said no more about it. But had my mind been morbid, it might have brought tears.   Had I already been aggravated, it would have only added vexation.   Such pathological cases of exaggerated sinful tendency in various directions, serve to illustrate much of the nature of sin in general.

With every person who knows good from evil, there are three stages to sin.

1. The presentation of the temptation.   The apple was in the Garden of Eden from the beginning, and our first parents were forbidden to eat it.   This very prohibition, doubtless, caused them to look at it, and possibly examine it through intellectual curiosity.   Then the serpent begins his allurement,—" Eat it.   It will do you no harm.   You will not die.   You see it is pleasing to the eye.   Why not as pleasing to the taste? "   How long these subtle arguments of the tempter continued before Eve actually desired to eat it, we cannot know.   We have many cases where temptation is in full view a long time before desire arises.   Some people, because of their peculiar character, training and physical make-up, are almost immune to certain temptations, and may live in the midst of them a long time without desiring them.   The same person may immediately desire some other evil if presented.   Certain appetites seem to develop in some people from heredity, without any provocation whatever in the individual.

2. The second stage begins with the faintest desire for the object of temptation. Desire may spring up spontaneously after more or less prolonged exposure to temptation, or may be hastened by some physical circumstance of seeming or imagined necessity, or an appeal to some inbred or acquired appetite. A man who had never stolen anything was seen carrying wood out of a yard when he was out of fuel. A young fellow who had always been honest, but rather a spendthrift, when out of money stole five dollars from his room-mate at school. A man of correct habits and tastes in every other line may indulge the sexual appetite with the least provocation or inducement. There are three great temptations,— pleasure, profit and preferment,— that are natural desires of mankind, and open up a wide entrance for temptations of many kinds. The world longs for a good time. People want, crave, and cherish wealth and honor. Any temptation that promises to gratify either of these desires, these mental predispositions, will soon awaken desire.

With the beginning of desire begins the actual moral battle. On the one side is the fancied picture of satisfaction gained from the object of temptation. On the other side is the condemning voice of conscience. The world today is money mad. Why? Some desire it for the pleasure they may enjoy from a frivolous expenditure of it.   Others see ahead of them a vision of fine homes and large bank accounts. Still others look forward to higher social standing and prestige in the community.   Here is presented a dishonest means of getting a large sum.   On the other hand is the moral sense that it is wrong.   It is sin.   It is deceitful.   It will weaken the character and start the soul to Hell. But there it is.   There are the results to be obtained from it.   I want it.   It will pay my bills.   It will show me a good time.   It will swell my bank account.   Oh, I want it.   And thus the battle may go on for days in the soul, as it vacillates between the two decisions.   A very small thing may finally decide it.   Some good, reading God's word, a sermon, meditation upon the life of some good man, a kind word from a friend, may gain hypertrophy of the attention long enough to get the mind off of sin and give right the victory.   Or some other rascal may say, " Take it," and the desire gains control of the dynamic center, and the soul rushes pellmell into ruin.

3. Then comes the actual fall.   In the preceding brief paragraph is couched in a few words the history of thousands of lost souls. Desire may linger, now almost strong enough for action, now vacillating, until often the slightest thing,— a word from some chum, some slight bodily disorder, or it may be simply the

accumulated strength of the many appeals of
the temptation as they linger in subconsciousness, together with another sudden and powerful
appeal of the temptation when the subject is off
guard, perhaps nothing of importance occupying the center of interest,— will cause the final
yielding to sin.

Of course the process is not so extended in
many cases.   In most cases these three steps are
enacted in rapid succession, and sin is committed immediately upon temptation.   This is
the case with most habitual sin, such as swearing, lying, and especially indulging in sinful
temper.   A man is angry the instant he is
provoked.   Some fellows strike in an instant.
A profane man swears upon provocation so
slight that he is unaware of it.   In many cases
the appeal to the sense of pleasure — pain —
seems to be the motive power back of sin.   Some
one has defined sin as mal-hypertrophy of attention.   This may not be the whole truth, especially in the more spontaneous sins.   But it
certainly covers the chief psychological explanation of the more deliberate transgression of the
law.   And even the more spontaneous sins
would not be committed if the attention were
fixed upon some good, and righteousness were
a fixed habit of life.

The first few times any sin is committed,
there is a feeling of remorse and condemnation

at the thought that one has acted contrary to his best judgment. The memories of the struggle are still fresh. But this sense of shame weakens with every succeeding commis-sion of the same evil, until the voice of conscience is silenced, and the soul becomes dead in tres-pass and sin. With this moral decline the in-terest in all good gradually decreases. The sinner cares less for the company of the right-eous, and seeks the company of his kind. He even shuns the company of good men, because of his sense of shame for sin, and the fear that they may chide him for his evil conduct. All these things only hasten the time when sin shall gain complete possession. With sin in the as-cendency, and all moral impressions delegated to the very perimeter of subconsciousness, years may pass without any thought of reform, and indeed with little sense of sin.

CHAPTER II

AWAKENING

The great problem of the church is the awakening of the soul that is dead in trespass and sin. The voice of conscience has become low or almost silent. The good impressions of youth are almost forgotten. If they come up unbidden, they are immediately cast off as unwelcome, for their coming brings a remorse that is unpleasant. The attention is immediately turned from them to some revery of frivolity and sin. Much of the sin committed is not so voluntary as habitual. The days of moral struggle are past, and sin is committed spontaneously at the first suggestion. All would-be impressions for good, not being in sympathy with the set habits of life and mental predisposition, fail to gain the attention. For psychologically, it is a problem of attention. As sin was mal-hypertrophy of attention, how shall right and a due sense of sin gain the attention and reach the dynamic center of psychic activity?

It is far more difficult to cause the person who has been enlightened from youth to realize a deep sense of sin, than one who has been in darkness.   The man who has heard the gospel truth all his life does not seem to heed it.   But preach the verities of sin and torment to one who has not heard a sermon for several years, and he is far more likely to be seriously impressed.

The majority of the first class do not listen with the attention that gives the gospel the center of active consciousness.   But the man who seldom hears the gospel listens with keen attention.   In many cases, before he is conscious of it everything else has slipped into oblivion, and the message has complete hypertrophy of the attention.   This man will remember far more of the sermon, and during the days immediately following, it will flit spontaneously through his mind and steal into his conversation.   If this man hears the gospel every day for a prolonged period, he may be brought to a decision.   Every message adds to his consciousness of sin, until it so completely absorbs the attention that it becomes a subject of constant meditation,— what Ribo calls " fixed attention."   He neither sleeps nor eats well. This complete absorption of the attention awakens the conviction and penitence and repentance, which will be considered in the next two chapters.

It is in the light of these tendencies that

Fairburn says,—" There is more hope of the conversion of the unclothed savage than of the clothed and skilled and inured wrong-doer of our east-end dens and our west-end clubs." This is altogether true. The heathen savage worships ignorantly, he knows not what. Deity is represented to him by various crude objects. He is often more scrupulous in the observance of his cruel rites than is civilized Christianity in the worship of Christ. He is anxious to learn about God, and welcomes any light on the subject. He is far more religious according to his knowledge than many Europeans or Americans. The problem of the teacher is not to make him religious, but to show him how to be religious.

But the subject we are considering is one who knows, or has the opportunity of knowing, God's will, but lacks the disposition to do it. Habitual evil has become the natural trend of life. The first problem is clearly that of good gaining the attention long enough to make a definite impression upon the consciousness. How shall the fact that he is a sinner and under the condemnation of sin, and that the joys of salvation await him for the asking, gain hypertrophy of attention long enough to reach the point of dynamogenesis?

In many cases attention must be forced by the obsession of something beyond the ordinary. A sudden death in the community, personal sickness, or sickness in the family, the moral reform of some intimate friend, some calamity or accident in the community, and many other such circumstances, will serve to break into the continuity of the attention that has thus far seemed armored against all thoughts of a moral nature. Fairburn says, " The most remarkable thing about suffering is not its extent of duration, its intensity or immensity, but its educative, regenerative and propulsive force, its power to make man conscious of his responsibilities, and awaken in him the desire to fulfil them. This is, if not its main function, its chief result." Prof. George Stephen says, " A sinful life at its most has something unstable about it, and is liable to be surprised and overthrown, because not sin, but righteousness, is the essence of the soul."

Sometimes the very effort to awaken the sinner only causes him to sin the more, by directing his attention to it. The very thought of evil may lay additional temptation. When we direct the thought to sin, let it be to its recklessness and its consequences, and this to contrast it with good. Contrast the misery of sin with the joys of salvation. Forgetting the things that are behind, we press towards the mark . . . of our high calling. " Whatsoever things are lovely, think on these things."

It is by no means necessary that one should experience the harsher obsessions spoken of above. There are times when one experiences what Mill calls a " dull state of nerves," as when extremely tired, or on awakening from sleep or revery, when there is no strong motive occupying the dynamic center of consciousness, that very slight occurrences will shift the center of psychic activity and awaken thoughts of good. If, perchance, the subject happens to read some good book, hear a message of God, fall into meditation upon some good life, and so forth, at such a time, it may start the thought in the direction of good, until after a while the attention becomes fixed upon it.

Peter heard the cock crow, and immediately the words of Jesus were brought to his mind and he was deeply penitent.

Dr. Munhall was awakened by the sound of a church bell one morning while he was in a saloon, ready to drink a glass of beer. Leaving the beer untouched, he left his companions and went home. He took out his Bible and read it, and upon his knees gave himself to God.

C. H. Yatman had not given Christ a thought for a long time, when suddenly one day his employer said, as he looked him in the face, " Will you be a Christian? " And he said, " Yes," and decided immediately.

A godly father and his son went into a restaurant, and when their meal was served he asked God's blessing just as he was accustomed to do at home. It so impressed two young men sitting near, as it brought up images of early training in godly homes, that both gave themselves to God.

Professor James tells of an Oxford graduate who, although the son of a preacher, had not entered a church for eight years, spending the money he earned at journalism, drinking and carousing. A lady friend sent him Drummond's " Natural Law in the Spiritual World," asking his opinion of it as a literary work only. He shut himself up in his room for a careful study of it. In a little while the words, " He that hath the Son hath life eternal, he that hath not the Son hath not life," fastened upon him. He realized himself alone with God, a sinner.

With the attention regained in the right direction, there is hope of moral reform. Thomas Carlyle passed this crisis of life while walking a dirty, filthy street. Count Tolstoy reached it through a series of meditations that stole upon him unbidden. So perplexed was he, that he had to hide the rope to keep from hanging himself. A study of the people who possessed the joys of salvation convinced him. Yet he vacillated between God and no God, now in joy, now in despair. Finally he compared his believing states with his doubting states, and, finding that he always had joy and light in faith, and darkness in doubt, he was confirmed in his belief in God. While these last decisions are rather of an intellectual type, they also illustrate the passing of the crisis in some lives as well.

There is a sort of natural liberal passive religion of an intellectual type that controls attention and diverts from all serious convictions. There is a belief that is merely mental, but worship is spiritual.

With the attention once diverted to religious thoughts, if given full liberty, the sinner's conviction will become deeper and deeper, until his sense of sinfulness will take full possession. I said, " if given full liberty," for in many lives conviction is driven away completely time after time before reaching dynamic strength. Temptations, evil associations, thoughts of severing friendships, and sacrificing pleasures necessary to a moral change, often interfere, and delay or destroy for the time all religious meditation.

But let us follow the psychic process on to the point of decision. The mind has now been directed toward good. The subject knows he is a sinner. The more he meditates upon his lifetime disobedience to God, the more ashamed of his life he is. Every sermon he hears, every good book he reads, every time he meets a good man, he feels his own depravity. Whenever there is the least stagnation in the stream of consciousness, this remorse for sin comes up. It fills the wakeful periods of night, and the leisure moments of the day. The accumulated force of all former impressions seems to be called forth from subconsciousness. Occasionally some circumstance,— impressions from a sermon or good reading, conversation of a friend, some accident or calamity,— will bring the subject very near to decision. There is more than one time in most lives when there is but a step between them and the kingdom of God. Some souls pass many such experiences. Prof. James says that many of our moral aspirations are only strong enough to reach a point just below dynamogenesis. But each of these moments helps to bring the sense of sin or conviction, as it is commonly called, to the point of fixed attention. There is now a greater battle than when sin first gained ascendency. There is a wavering first to the right, then to the evil, for days and weeks, and sometimes even months,— now almost determined, then weakened in the determination,— until suddenly in one of the better moments a little obsession from without, or sometimes just a little deeper thought on sin, brings the sinner to penitence. The longer the decision is delayed, the more powerful the concentration of the psychic forces upon this one thing as the object of fixed attention, and the greater the agony.   Many persons scarcely eat or sleep.

As this goes on from day to day, the mind is in a morbid state, combining a deep sense of sin, a sense of God's displeasure, and a horror of the dreadful consequences of sin.   Sometimes the soul sinks into a state of melancholia and is subject to all kinds of illusions, accompanied by corresponding bodily reactions.   The least pain or bodily disorder is greatly magnified, as the attention is riveted upon the sense of sinfulness, the uncertainty of life and the certainty of death.   This one subject fills the thoughts of day and the dreams of night.   I heard of one man who dreamed that at sunrise he was to die. On awakening he summoned his doctor, who on making a very careful examination found every organ in healthy condition save that the patient was very nervous.   The fact is that he was troubled about his lost soul, and afraid he would die unsaved.

It was in the midst of this struggle that Freeborn Garretson got off his horse and prayed that God allow him to postpone the matter until a more convenient season.   But when he mounted his steed again he was troubled more than ever, until, dropping the reins on the horse's neck and throwing up his hands, he cried,—" Lord Jesus, I submit."

It was in this period of struggle that Benjamin Abbott wished to kill himself because he was so troubled.   Being deterred by conscience, he jumped into his wagon and drove home at full speed thinking the Devil was after him.   He was so frightened that his hair stood up on his head.

The psychic effect of this shifting of the dynamic center was very marked in many of the early converts.   The early church history of this country abounds in stories of people struck dumb for the time, some fainting to the floor, some frightened almost into madness, when the thought that they were lost sinners first fastened itself upon them.

CHAPTER III

PENITENCE AND REPENTANCE

In the last chapter, the deep sense of sin had brought the mind to a morbid state of extreme unrest. In this terrible anxiety, all kinds of diversions are resorted to, to relieve the mind and soul of its agony. Some have gone insane under the intense pressure of conviction of sin. Others have pined away their strength. Yet others have endured all sorts of penance to rid their souls of this awful burden, all to no avail. But here come the words of Christ,—" Repent." " Whosoever will come after me, let him deny himself, take up his cross and follow me." Repentance may be humiliating from a human view. The cross may be heavy. The breaking off of old habits and associations may be hard. But, as with Bunyan's pilgrim, the longer the mind continues in this morbid state, the heavier seems the load. Continued fixed attention upon sin brings a deeper realization of its heinousness.

It may be well for some people to suffer

this agony for a little while. It may make them more zealous in their faith and good works in after years. Finally the soul reaches a state similar to Peter's when he was about to sink while trying to walk on the water, so terrible seems the danger from sin. When the soul reaches this point,—"Lord, save or I perish; I will do anything, Lord, to get rid of this burden," it is ready for God to enter.

Now while this morbid state of deep conviction is necessary to cause the sinner to feel his moral imperfection, his lack of sympathy with God and His law, sometimes this very fixed attention upon sin delays the work of faith. It holds such complete hypertrophy of attention that the soul is so intent upon introspection that it fails to see the offered mercy of God.

I have seen persons pray day and night for a long time, having relinquished every worldly habit and practise,— to use the evangelical term, having made the complete surrender. But the mind could not be diverted from its extreme morbidness long enough to consider offered mercy. I know a woman who has been a penitent for years, the morbid state never having been lifted sufficiently for her to get a firm hold upon God by faith.

A classic example of extreme morbidness is Suso, a German mystic of the fourteenth century. He wore for a long time a hair shirt and an iron chain, until the blood ran from him, so that he had to leave it off. He had an undergarment made for him with strips of leather into which a hundred and fifty nails were driven. In this he used to sleep. This, together with the lice, with which most medieval monks were infested, made him squirm sometimes like a worm. Then he had two leather loops made by which he fastened his hands beside his throat. When this threatened to permanently injure his arms, he had two leather gloves made with sharp tacks in them, so that if he should smack at the lice in his sleep, he would tear his flesh with the tacks. He continued this for about sixteen years. Later he made a cross with thirty protruding needles and nails, which he wore on his back night and day. Sometimes he would do penance by striking himself on the back, making the wounds deeper. At this same time he procured an old door upon which he slept at night. He practised such rigid poverty that he would not even touch a penny. All these and many other tortures he suffered to emulate the sorrows of his crucified Lord.

Of course this was a distinctly pathological case. He continued thus until after forty years old, when God's good pleasure was revealed to him in a dream. Many a soul goes on and on, bemoaning sin and guilt a long time, until some obsession from without causes him to stop and think long enough to realize that it is not God's will that he should perish, but live; or it may be that some promise already in subconsciousness suddenly bubbles into active psychosis.

We as Christians have no patent on these experiences, for all religions have a sense of conviction, followed by some sort of propitiation or repentance before conversion. There is little difference between Suso described above, and the Hindu devotee who measures his length to a distant shrine, or who stretches prostrate under the tropical sun on a board of nails, to appease Deity. While we are endeavoring to trace the psychological aspects of Christian experience, we are describing the mental states which pertain to all religions.

This agony of repentance, doctrinally is the old man dying, being crucified, making way for the new birth. Paul said,—"I am crucified with Christ; nevertheless I live, yet no longer I, but Christ liveth in me." Psychologically, it is a morbid state into which the soul has sunken from continued fixed attention upon the lost state in sin.

Thus far I have been delineating the experiences of those who come under the teaching and influence of the evangelical denominations.   But there are other Christian faiths, of the more liberal and formal type, who rely more upon the sacrament and ceremonial.   In these the deep sense of sin and depravity is not given so much accent.   Men are taught to stop evil, do good, and attend the sacraments and other Christian duties.   With these the mind never sinks into such morbidness.   There is simply a voluntary focusing of the attention upon the intended reformed life.   Wicked habits and thoughts are driven into subconsciousness.   It is more of an intellectual process, and does not so thoroughly absorb the whole being.   In many cases there is a total reliance upon the church and the sacraments, with little or no change in the habits.   There has been no shifting of the dynamic center of psychosis.   There has been no change of the habitual center of interest.   There has only been an intellectual assent to certain doctrines of the church. These souls, believing as they have been taught, that this is all that is necessary, are as contented as, and in many cases more so than, those who have experienced a deeper work of grace.   While the extreme morbid state may not be absolutely necessary, it is a powerful aid in forgetting old habits of thought and action, and focusing attention on new ones.   Many of those whose change has been free from the morbid, are just as good morally as those who have passed through extreme morbidness. The intellect is completely focused on the new life. And the determined soul voluntarily coneentrates attention upon good and voluntarily keeps it turned from evil, until it becomes a habit of life. Where there is less struggle in the change, there is usually more effort required to maintain the purity desired. This is what Starbuck, as we shall see later, calls a " volitional type of religion."

CHAPTER IV

CONVERSION AND REGENERATION

The shifting of the dynamic center of psychic action from this morbid state to one of optimism, where the soul believes he receives the things for which he asks, is not always easy. The obsession of some outer influence is often necessary to break the continuity of attention upon the morbid state, and give faith a chance.

I know a man who, after continuing in this morbid state for many days, sometimes almost despairing, was taught the lesson of faith by his horse. He went into the stable one morning to feed the horse. As he opened the feed chest, the horse began to neigh in expectancy. The thought broke upon him suddenly,— " Why, even that horse has faith in me. Why, look how confidently he expects his feed as soon as I open the feed chest. Yet I have waited at the mercy seat many days." And immediately he believed.

Every student of religious history remembers the history of Luther's enlightenment. While ascending the Cathedral steps, kneeling in prayer on each as he went, suddenly the words, " The just shall live by faith," sprang up from subconsciousness and took complete possession of his attention. And the light came immediately.

The religion of Jesus Christ is, more than any other, a religion of pure faith. Christ told his disciples,—" Whatsoever things ye desire, when ye pray, believe that ye receive them, and ye shall receive them." (Mark 11:24.) Belief in prayer and its efficacy helps one to believe that he receives the things for which he prays. This is an entirely new attitude to the inexperienced mind. In practical life, we depend on sight as we go. We walk by sight, work by sight, and, in a word, live by sight. It is a fact, however, that sight continued loses its vividness, but faith continued becomes clearer. And in all religion we live — and, in fact, do all things — by faith. It is a long time before some minds can so completely change what has hitherto been the set habit of life. Thus far I have treated it as dawning upon the subject suddenly, but this is by no means necessary. The predisposition of a mind that has depended upon sight is difficult to overcome. See how long it took the disciples to understand Christ's ministry. It was not because they were not attentive to his teaching. But their preconceived idea of Christ

setting up an earthly kingdom kept their minds
blinded to the true nature of his mission.

There are many today upon whom the light
gradually dawns. Even with many of these,
their realization of it is sudden. Professor
James says, "Where there is a pronounced
emotional sensibility, a tendency to automa-
tism, and suggestibility of a passive type, there
will be a sudden conversion."

Now conversion, in its generally accepted
sense, includes not only this acceptance of
God's promises,— which after all may be, and
sadly in some cases is, a mere intellectual
process,— but regeneration, being born again.
"If any man be in Christ, he is a new creature;
old things have passed away and all things become new."

Caird said, "Oneness of the mind and will
with the divine mind and will is not the future
hope and aim of religion, but its very beginning and birth in the soul." Psychologically,
this will require a complete unification of the
mental self, and a shifting of the habitual center of dynamic psychosis, or what James calls
the "habitual center of personal energy." It
is not always easy to follow these psychic
changes. The subject himself cannot. Much
of it goes on in the subconscious or subliminal
self.

The mental energy, until now divided among the many issues of life, is centered upon this one thing.   The whole mind is focused on a unification of the self with the divine will.   The suddenness with which the whole emotional self is involved, itself makes the experience deeper and more lasting.   It is the suddenness of all emotion that makes it take such full possession of the whole mind, whether it be joy, anger, love, hatred or disappointment.

Dr. Starbuck distinguishes two kinds of conversion,— a volitional type, and a type by self-surrender.   In the first type the regenerative change is gradual.   In the latter it is sudden. But, after all, this is a distinction rather of degree than of kind.   In the first class there is a gradual building up of character, building a new moral and spiritual self, piece by piece. But even here, as in education in any practical accomplishment, growth is not steady, but by leaps and starts.   But in the development of Christianity more and more stress has been laid upon self-surrender as the vital turning point in spiritual life.

This complete self-surrender is reached in two ways.   The only way to exterminate any emotion is to kill it with its opposite, or else just wear it out.   Sometimes a sense of saving faith suddenly seizes the attention; whether it be from the obsession of something from without or the sudden springing up of thought from subconsciousness, it matters not.

The suddenness with which the center of psychosis is shifted excites the whole self. If the subject is of an emotional nature, he will surely become demonstrative. But we reserve the treatment of the emotional side for a separate chapter.

There are many who continue in the morbid state of consciousness, praying, meditating, weeping, and so forth, until they simply wear it out. I have fresh in memory a woman who was recently converted in my church. She was deeply penitent, and had " earnestly' groaned for redemption " several days, until one night I noticed this seemed to die away. She seemed dazed for the space of fifteen or twenty minutes, when suddenly she burst forth, " Praise God, I am saved." As the morbidness died out, it left a void for faith to enter.

Now while the soul has been struggling in penitence, the mind has been focusing upon this one thing, and the new center of personal energy is being subconsciously incubated.

While, theologically, there is no necessity for a prolonged struggle, it has certain psychological advantages. It takes time for the mind that has harbored evil thoughts of all sorts, and much of the time given evil the dynamic center of psychosis, to completely lose these evil thoughts in subconsciousness and give repentance the arena of attention. The anxiety about the intended moral reform and the continued agony of penitence, filling the mind for a period of time, helps the consuetudinary evil-mindedness to be lost in the subliminal self. The continued reflection upon the consequences of sin and the anguish it is causing us, engenders a hatred of all sinful thought and action. This complete disgust and hatred of sin is necessary in order that the affections and cravings may be completely centered upon righteousness. The memory of the struggle that sin caused will be an incentive to abhor sin and turn a deaf ear to temptation in the future. If, indeed, the man in Christ is a new creature, old things having passed away and all things become new, there surely must be a complete revolution of psychic habits. There must be new desires, appetites, aims and inspirations. Much as the emotional side of religious experience is discredited, the emotions are the dynamic force in many lives. There are some lives in which any motive or sentiment, to be effective or lasting, must arouse and completely involve the emotional self. The arousing of the emotions helps to complete the eradication of old desires, and rivets the attention more completely upon the new life. For we must remember that thought is ever a source of action. If the life is changed, it is because the predominating thoughts are different. The life of this world is a life of self. But in the Christian, self is lost in Christ, and thoughts of self and selfish aims give way to the imitation of Christ's life. When Wilberforce was so intent upon the liberation of slaves, some one said to him, "I hope in your efforts for the welfare of others, you will not forget your own soul." "Why," said he, "I forgot I had a soul." So the Christian's whole self is lost in his work for Christ.

Harold Begbie, in that wonderful little book, "Souls in Action," tells about a dipsomaniac woman who passed through a long season of repentance. But when we read her whole history we can better understand it. She had been an active Christian worker, especially active in temperance work. But there was the hereditary taste for drink in the family. After ten years of active Christian service, she fell into sin, but all the while kept up the outward appearance of righteousness. What a hypocrite she was. She had learned to lie, drink and steal. One night she went to hear Hugh Price Hughs. The sermon struck her to her very heart's core. The next day she went to the preacher's home, but he being busy, Mrs. Hughs comforted and advised her. The woman seemed deeply penitent, and came often for advice. But it was some time yet before she was penitent enough to stop drinking. It took a long time for her to reach the full surrender, although it may have been in subconscious incubation all the time.

It is necessary for a soul to become so completely tired of sin and disgusted with its shame that the dynamic forces of the mind be so completely reversed and directed against the old sinful habits as to be able to resist temptations as they come in after life.

The Oxford graduate, spoken of in the last chapter, became exposed to the temptation to drink the next day after he was converted, and again took too much. His sister despaired that he had taken too much and had fallen already. But he went to his room so completely disgusted with himself that he again wrestled with God for a season, and from that time he never desired drink. Now every highly emotional state is followed by a state more or less stupid, when the emotion gradually wears out. This man's mind had not yet become permanently settled and unified in the new life. As the emotional state following his conversion gradually wore out, with the old life yet lingering fresh in subconsciousness, it was easy for the old habit to gain full possession. But this first experience aroused his determination for a stronger voluntary concentration of the attention upon the new life he expected to live. With this complete shifting of the center of mental energy, the desire for drink left him, never to return.

" Conversion," writes Joseph Allein, the Puritan, " is not the putting in a patch of holiness, but with the true convert holiness is woven into all his powers, principles and practises."

We are all automatons to some extent, and when righteousness becomes the set principle of life, godly habits are formed, and we do the right and reject the wrong with ease and comfort. Of course there are crises in every life when there is a struggle to conquer temptation. One man was about to be ruined under the stress of severe temptation in his weakest place, when Christ's words, " My grace is sufficient," came up in his mind, and he walked away calmly. " Be not overcome with evil, but overcome evil with good," that is the remedy. The psychological explanation of all this is,— if good has the whole attention, evil has little chance.

CHAPTER V

DEVELOPMENT OF CHRISTIAN STRENGTH

The new-born soul is a stranger in a strange land. He must learn an entirely new system of habits of thought and action. Upon his conversion, one feels that he could conquer a whole world of sin. His whole nature is saturated with the change. But when the excitement abates and the emotions calm down, he finds that some of the old habits of thought are not completely exterminated, but are only relegated to subconsciousness, to reappear, often at the least expected moment. Paul said — "When I would do good, evil is present with me." Evil thought is the forerunner of evil deeds. The problem with every Christian is to get rid of the evil thoughts that produce evil deeds.

Now there is a trace in the subconsciousness of every thought and deed of life. The more frequently evil thoughts gain attention, the more vivid they become. On the other hand, the more completely they can be kept out of the active psychosis, the less vivid they are and the less frequently they will recur.

The great problem, then, psychologically considered, is control of attention. The mind must not be allowed to rest on things that are evil. I have said many times that I wish I could give every convert a definite Christian work to perform, upon which he would center his ambition sufficiently so that his mind would be upon that during every idle moment, so as to keep the active consciousness busy. It is usually during the moments when there is nothing of importance occupying the habitual center of interest, and subconsciousness has sway, that old cravings arise. "An idle mind is the devil's workshop."

A young man went to a minister and besought him for a remedy for evil thoughts. "Why," said the fellow, "my mind is almost constantly filled with the vilest thoughts. I fear that in some unguarded moment I may be led into sin by them." The preacher told him to buy a cheap copy of the New Testament, tear some leaves from it and place a few in each pocket. "Now," said he, "whenever an evil thought arises, take out a leaf and read a verse. You can do that, no matter where you are. Keep saying it over and over, until you have committed it to memory. By that time your evil thought will be gone." The fellow tried it, and in two months' time he was not only cured of his trouble, but from the frequent meditation upon God's word, religion had gained almost complete hypertrophy of his attention. He had a keener sense of sin, and a greater love for all good.

Now what is the philosophy of all this? Habitual study of these passages of the Word had kept the attention centered on religion. Evil thoughts, not being allowed attention, were gradually forgotten. During the early Christian life, and to some extent throughout life, there must be some voluntary control of the attention. As the years go by, righteous habits will be formed that will make it easier to be good, but there must always be a will exercised in that direction.

But what shall I say about the more impulsive natures that fly off in temper or profanity in an instant, without any time to think? These are the more difficult sins to conquer. There is little psychic activity connected with the deed. High tempered people are usually good automatons, and controlled by subconsciousness. Yet if the attention is powerfully focused on this weakness, it can be gradually conquered by them.

If we believe God's Word, we believe that His grace is sufficient for all needs. And if our attention can be controlled sufficiently to hold the act in check for a minute, the evil act will not usually be committed. Sometimes things incubated in subconsciousness will burst forth upon the active consciousness with explosive force, and one is often surprised at the things he will do upon such occasions. If, when one is seized with such a sudden impulse, he would stop long enough to pray, " God help me," two things would happen: Grace would be supplied, and the attention would be turned from the sin to God.

All the good things heard and read cannot always be in the center of attention. They are not all remembered. But if those remembered could be mustered enmasse at will, what a strong fortress would shield us from the power of temptation! But we do retain a trace of every good seen, heard, or read, in at least two ways. (a) Focusing the attention upon good for the time, turns it from evil and aids in forming the habit of righteous thought. The more completely the thought had hypertrophy of the attention, the more frequently it will recur during the hours and days immediately following. (b) There will remain a trace or fragment of it in subconsciousness. I maintain that no influence for good is entirely lost. There is a trace of it all remaining in subconsciousness. It may not show forth at the time, but the accumulated force of previous moral

impressions does break forth some time. Much
of our daily performance is not governed by
thought at all, but by subconsciousness, au-
tomatism, habit. And every outward influence
leaves its mark upon the subliminal self. My
moral character now is the accumulated force
of all previous influences as they remain today
in subconsciousness. This is part of the process of sanctification. This is a term used in
three distinct ways. 1. It is the process of
being made holy. 2. It is the point where
one will not willingly and voluntarily trans-
gress God's law. 3. It is absolute perfection.
I use the term here in the first sense, according
to its etymology. It is the process of growing in grace toward holiness, growing like
Christ, from continued attention, meditation
upon Him, and imitation of Him. Psychologically, it is the continued concentration of
the attention upon right conduct according to
God's law until godliness gains such complete
hypertrophy of the attention that all things
are measured by a standard of right and
wrong. To this end, voluntary control of the
attention is sought, so that when evil comes up
in the mind, it is banished at once and the
mind is immediately fixed upon some good. In
this way one is brought to sanctification in its
second sense, when righteousness completely
controls the center of interest. Absolute per-

fection might here be attained if the whole subliminal self were separated from us.   Some at
this stage are deluded into a belief that they
are absolutely perfect and cannot possibly sin.
Those who have been carefully observant of
such lives find that even this delusion helps to
keep the mind off of sin, but still imperfections
crop out.   The subject may not be conscious
of them, for his very delusion leads him to believe that what he thinks and does is right.
He ignores the fact that his mind and judgment are still imperfect.   Perfection here might
be possible if subconsciousness never broke in
upon the active self after the habitual center
of interest has been changed, the dynamic center of psychosis shifted.   But if this subconscious self were dead, memory would be gone,
experience set at nought, and indeed the whole
former life would be a forgotten dream.   If a
man reached a state where he could not sin,
there would no longer be any moral quality to
his acts.   It is in the voluntary refusal to sin
that the soul has its moral quality and strength.
The *idea* of absolute perfection has, however,
its function in Christian life, as a goal toward
which we aim, not as already attained, but,
like Paul, we press forward towards the mark.
The more perfection, Christlikeness, occupies
the attention, the more this ideal will control
the attention.   It will not only be occupying

the habitual center of interest, the dynamic center of psychosis, but its imprint will be left deeper and deeper upon subconsciousness.

From what has been said, one might suppose the development of Christian strength was a steady process. But it is not. The stream of consciousness is not a steady flow at all, neither is the development of Christian strength steady, but by spasms and paroxysms. There are periods when the stream of consciousness, the flow of psychic activity, is quite smooth. But the greater advances are made by occasional leaps. These leaps forward are either from obsessions from without, or from meditation,— voluntary concentration of the attention upon the promotion of holiness. Repeated attention to any subject clarifies the field of consciousness and facilitates discrimination in that particular line. Hence the discrimination of sin becomes more acute. And there is nothing that so completely designates the moral quality of a man as his sense of sin. Of course this may be carried to an extreme, and become asceticism on the one hand, or extreme morbidness — until the subject becomes theopathetic — on the other hand.

If the convert is indeed a new man, with the habitual center of interest completely shifted, it should affect the whole mental life. The ideal is the Christ-Life. We keep an image of his life of purity before us. The sentiments are completely changed to conform to the new ideal. Old appetites and desires are crowded out by the new ones upon which attention has been voluntarily fixed. Fancy pictures the time when we shall have conquered the lusts of the flesh, the lusts of the eye and the pride of life. The fleshly impulses have given way to the one burning desire to please God. We seize with avidity anything that will help to promote this one central desire. The imagination that used to be busy manufacturing all kinds of wickedness is now contemplating the joys of salvation and the glories beyond. Every faculty of the mental self is alive to the change. All this focusing of the mental self upon righteousness helps to conquer the old self and increase the spiritual strength.

As the ideas, desires, sentiments and ambitions are unified and fixed upon the new life, they will have more and more effect upon those habits which are not the subject of thought. As subconsciousness is more completely permeated with the new life, we form habits of right doing, and refuse the wrong with much less effort than before. Just as conation was predisposed to the gratification of self before, now it becomes more and more disposed to godliness. I am becoming thoroughly persuaded that the greatest source of strength is activity. The

more we work for the spread of God's kingdom, the stronger we become in His service.
It must be so, for where there is great effort
expended, there is great desire for success.
The sentiments are centered upon it completely.

We become enthusiastic over it.   The emotions are stirred in its favor. All these va-
ried mental activities help to fix the mind more
firmly upon the new life.

Of course there are times when, even though
we have done all in human power by the aid of
divine grace, we will have rough sailing.
When the moral struggles of life come, we are
shown how weak we are, and yet how strong
with the assistance of God's grace. When we
are obsessed with some evil allurement, the fa-
cility with which we refuse to yield will depend
upon how completely the habitual center of interest has been shifted. If the mind is centered upon the service of God and fellow man,
busy with planning and contemplating some
good, there is little chance for evil to gain sufficient attention to reach dynamic force.

Then there are allurements that come upon
us gradually. We are a busy people in a busy
age. And business is sometimes allowed to
interfere with religion. " Take time to be
holy " is a necessary precaution for many.
When the neglect of some duty will afford a
few needed minutes for business, it is easy to

neglect just this one time. But every such neglect gains for business a part of the attention that belongs to religion. But a few such neglects weaken the righteous habit and begin a habit of neglect. Or there may be presented a slightly dishonest proposition whereby gain may be obtained, or some morally unhealthy amusement from which momentary pleasure may be obtained, or some allurement of the sinful lusts of the flesh. Now if the dynamic center of psychic activity is constantly and completely occupied with good, the thought of these things will be immediately turned aside. But every minute attention is usurped from good by evil thoughts, the mind's grip upon good weakens, and evil is that much nearer the victory. If, happily, the soul is strong enough and sufficiently intent upon the pursuit of the Christ-life as the ideal, the temptations will not gain sufficient attention for dynamogenesis, but will be voluntarily turned aside. And " Each victory will help you some other to win." Each time these evil temptations are refused attention, will cause them to have less claim on the attention the next time. While the mind turns aside to think of them it is wavering and weakening in godly integrity; but if good gains the victory, the soul takes a leap in advance. Every time sin is refused attention, we help to bring to pass the time when sin will not gain attention at all.

One of the most noticeable characteristics of those whose attention has been fixed upon godliness and whose habits have been formed in accordance with the complete shifting of the habitual center of interest, is their calmness in danger and trouble. When John Wesley was on his first voyage to America, he was astonished at the calmness of the Moravians on board during a storm. It made such a profound impression upon him that it awakened in him a desire for such peace.

Again, this was clearly a question of attention. Those Moravians were so thoroughly convinced of God's loving care and protection that they were satisfied that they would suffer no harm. Thus their attention was so completely occupied with their intimate relationship with God that they did not heed the storm. Take Peter for an example, when he tried to walk on the water. He did very well as long as he kept his eyes fixed upon Jesus. But when he heard the waves, that they were boisterous, he began to sink. The reason trouble does not trouble a Christian is that his mind is so completely occupied with the contemplation of God's love and mercy that he refuses trouble room in his attention. In affliction he is calm, because he knows that all these light afflictions will work out for him a far more and exceeding and eternal weight of glory. His attention is on the glory promised, and not on the affliction. The disagreeable circumstances that almost worry the world crazy, only obtain from the Christian passing notice, because he is too busy with the service of his God and the contemplation of eternal glory. This is the psychology of Christian happiness. Trouble cannot gain a hold upon the attention, for it is preoccupied with God's love. This is what enabled the martyrs to die, singing God's praises, ignoring the pains of death. The prospective glory of eternal bliss so completely filled the mind that even the tortures of the stake failed to gain attention, for the eye of faith saw far ahead in the way.

Everyone who has had any experience with the sick has noticed the patience and resignation of the believer in contrast with the restlessness and fear of the unconverted. When the unsaved man becomes very ill, if he thinks he will die, the thought of dying without Christ fills him with horror and consternation. The Christian bears the pains of body, looking forward to the day when he shall be freed from the body to be with God. When death comes, his attention is so completely fixed upon things beyond that, forgetting the body entirely, he

actually professes to gain a glimpse of the beyond.   Realizing that the end is near, the attention that has been fixed upon Jesus now refuses any place to the things of this world, and
sees only Jesus even before leaving the body.

CHAPTER VI

APOSTASY

In the last chapter we followed the moral struggle to a victory. But it does not always result that way. The longer the evil temptation holds the attention, the weaker becomes one's moral resistance. Much that was said in the chapter on sin might here be repeated. For the mental experience of a fall from grace is much the same as that during the first falling into sin against one's better judgment. We are creatures of habit in spiritual as well as physical life. How strong the temptation, or how long it shall endure before it gains the undivided attention, will depend upon how well the subject has gained control of the attention, and how firmly fixed is the habit of concentrating attention upon good. If the soul has had years of experience in turning the attention immediately away from the presentation of evil, there must usually be something abnormal or extraordinary about the temptation itself, or the manner of its presentation, or else it would not be noticed. There are times when we may be caught off guard. When there is nothing of importance occupying the attention, any obsession, whether good or evil, can obtain attention for a short time. If evil thus gains attention, one whose set principles of life are righteousness will immediately voluntarily turn the attention away from it. But suppose he does not turn attention away from it, although his set principles of life are against such actions, his judgment is prejudiced against such actions. Then there is the possible disgrace, the ridicule of his neighbors, and the frown of God. But all the time the possible enjoyment or profit is before the mind. The longer he continues to think about it, the more alluring it becomes, as it gains the attention more completely, forcing all arguments against it into the background. All this time the fleshly lusts of the body are urging participation in the evil presented. The longer the struggle continues, the firmer hold evil gains upon the attention, and the weaker all deterring influences. There may be additional obsession from without, or a sudden impulse from within, that hastens the final decision. The mental life is not at all a steady stream. There is frequently a leap into action.

While the above is about the usual process of fall into the more deliberate sins, I suspect the first steps toward fall are more frequently those sins committed on the impulse of the moment. Life is filled with provocations and adversities which cause one's temper to rise. Thousands indulge in those sins which are due to the indulgence of sinful temper, who will not commit the more deliberate sins. The suddenness of evil temper captures the attention that would be voluntarily refused the more deliberate appeals of the lusts of the flesh. Any impulse, whether good or evil, grows rapidly. Its very dynamic nature makes it grow by leaps and bounds. What today is attraction, tomorrow is love. What today is but a little dislike, tomorrow may be bitter hatred. The longer one thinks upon a wrong done him, the more angry he becomes. It takes but a short time, in the lives of the more sanguine natures, for this sinful hatred to gain such complete hypertrophy of attention that reason is for the time dethroned. Some men allow themselves to act like maniacs when they are angry.

Another prolific means of fall is the sudden presentation of the object of an old appetite at a time when one is physiologically in shape for it to appeal to the needs of the body. For example, there are times in the life of the converted drunkard, especially during his early Christian life, when upon the sudden and unexpected presentation of the temptation,— especially in the company and environment in which he used to drink,— he might take a drink before he thought. But if he had stopped to think, he would not have taken it.

Much of the success of the Christian life depends on how completely the center of interest was shifted in the beginning, and how completely the attention is fixed upon the pursuit of godliness. There are so many things that will usurp the attention belonging to religion. We are living in a very intensive business age. In the keenness of competition, there are so many tricks of business that will dull the spiritual sensitiveness. Everyone has an ambition to succeed. Little crooked methods are often presented whereby one may gain a point unseen and undiscovered. Now if the temporary interest in business is greater than the interest in the right, or if the habitual center of interest is divided, evil may get the right of way.

While attendance upon public worship may not be absolutely necessary, the concentration of the attention for an hour or so, one or more times each week, in the exclusive associations of the sanctuary, upon religion, is a powerful stimulus and aid to godliness. Those accustomed to it miss its hallowed influence when deprived of it. But here is a man who allows a business interest or engagement to prevent his attendance upon worship for a few weeks. It is remarkable how quickly the center of interest will begin to shift from church to business. The same would be true with the temporary neglect of any other duty. If this go on, before the subject is aware of it he has lost all interest in church, and business has completely absorbed his attention.

Another easy road to sin is through one's associates. We hear much nowadays about mass movements, public conscience, etcetera, and there is a bit of good psychology in such phrases. There is a contagion about human behaviour that cannot be ignored. There is good philosophy in that old hymn, " Shun evil companions." Many centuries ago Meander wrote, " Evil communications corrupt good manners." The truth of this was so evident that it was one of the few pagan maxims quoted by St. Paul. If the man who is trying to live a godly life is in the exclusive company of those of like ambition, their common aim will help to keep their minds centered upon right. When an evil thought is presented to one, another may have a song upon his lips, or the conversation of the crowd may be upon some healthful moral subject, so that the mind will be immediately turned away from the evil before it reaches the dynamic center of psychosis. But if at such a time the associations be evil, indulging in evil conversation or idle or profane gossip, the evil obsession will have an excellent opportunity to gain dynamic force. Then there will be the sense of shame and impropriety that will prevent one's doing evil, even if it reached that stage of desire in the midst of godly associates, while among evil people one will be encouraged to commit evil.

There is something about human nature that makes us go with the crowd. This is all the more powerful if the shifting of the habitual center of interest has not been complete. If the original fleshly desires and appetites have not been expelled from the active consciousness, and kept out, it is easy for evil,— already having a foundation in consciousness,— to gain dynamic control of the attention, when wicked environment helps to keep good out of the mind. When the crowd indulges in anything, there is a bit of sociability about us that makes us join in. We draw back from the conspicuity of being the only one to abstain. But if one is sufficiently established in right as a set and unalterable principle of life, he will not only abstain, but will pride himself in the conspicuity of his firmness. But many a weakling starts on the road to ruin in this way. It is painful for the young convert to cut off old associations, but it is often necessary. You may be ever so sincere, but you can no more free yourself from your environment than from the air you breathe.

There are many of the so-called innocent pleasures of life that harm the soul by usurping too much of the attention.   There may be little harm in any of the so-called diversions of the day, such as the various games of chance, or an occasional parlor dance with friends, but everyone acknowledges that they become very fascinating.   At first this is not noticed, but there grows up a strong impulse of desire for them to the exclusion of more healthful diversions.   The same might be said of much that is presented upon the modern stage.   Our cheap theatres, dime museums and picture shows do not in most cases aim at the instruction and elevation of society.   But the detective stories, lewd dances, and sickening love episodes with their elopements, are all calculated to appeal to the lower nature of men, the bodily lust, and animal passions and desires.   Unnoticed at first, the mind gradually drifts from all that is good and is filled with this vile stuff continually. None of these things develop intellect or stimulate culture.   They only appeal to the worldly desires of the flesh and gradually usurp the hypertrophy of attention belonging to religion. There may be little harm in the things themselves, but harm comes in the end from this mal-hypertrophy of the attention.

Whatever the sin, and whatever the inducement to commit it, and the manner in which it was committed, the first sin leaves an open door for the second. If it was committed after deliberation, there will be less deliberation the next time. If of the impulsive type, less provocation will be required each succeeding time. After the deed is done, conscience,— that voice of our better judgment according to the best light we possess,— condemns us. A feeling of shame comes over the subject when he meets some one who saw the sin committed, or knows of it. There is a feeling of disgust at the self for its foolishness and weakness. There is often a tendency to shun good people for fear of some possible reproof.

Much of the future of that soul depends upon the action of his associates at this time. A little encouragement in the right direction, a little well-expressed sympathy, may cause him to press with renewed vigor to regain the lost ground. A little scoffing and sneering while the mind is in this unsettled and confused condition may cause one to become so discouraged that he will have little courage to try to do right. In this state of discouragement, what control one might have of his attention is scarcely exercised. A little introspection at this time will cause some to make a desperate effort to regain the lost self-control. With others, introspection will only add despair to discouragement. Sometimes despair for a season will awake a sense of need, when a slight obsession for good will open the way for grace. But more frequently despair is but the beginning of the end. There were Christian and Hopeful in doubting castle of Giant Despair. Had not Hopeful thought of the key of faith in his bosom, both were nearing the end.

The one great enemy of faith is doubt. Faith is the great foundation principle of Christianity. There are many things, not clear to reason, that are made clear by faith. Faith makes clear a thousand difficulties of the unbelieving mind.   But let the mind once begin to doubt; let the attention once be diverted from faith, and begin to question its verities; let reason try to solve the mysteries of the Infinite; and doubt will soon have possession of the attention.   Believers can sink into agnostics and infidels.   A good example is the counter conversion of Jouffrey.   In spite of his vain endeavor to cling to the shipwreck of faith, doubt gained full sway.   When he realized that faith was gone, it was the saddest day of his life, as he found his old assurances gone and himself a confirmed infidel.   Few may sink so far, but sin and doubt are deadly to faith.

Finally, the soul says, " What is the use? I am making a failure of the whole business. I no longer enjoy the things of God.   Prayer has become a mere performance.   I am not good and everybody knows it." And here he ceases any effort to center the attention upon good and gives way to evil, giving it full chance at his attention, and often the last state of such a soul is worse than the first.

CHAPTER VII

THE EMOTIONS IN RELIGIOUS LIFE

There is no part of the mental self so prominent in many as the emotions. Persons of a
high strung, nervous temperament are usually
more emotional on any occasion than those of
a more phlegmatic trend. When the interests
are few and the education limited, the emotions
are usually more dominant, and more demonstrative in their expression. Now the emotional self as displayed in religion is not very
different from that displayed in any other
phase of life. In those branches of the church
where a deep sense of sin is not emphasized, and
consequently not so deep a sense of deliverance,
and often not so complete a shifting of the dy-
namie center, the emotions are not brought into
play so noticeably. The emotions are first
brought into action when the soul is awakened
to a deep sense of sin. The less conscious the
subject has been of sin before, the more marked
the effect upon the emotions when he is awakened to a sense of his lost condition. This ex-
plains the extreme action of some of the fron-

tiersmen, who had not heard a sermon or given religion a thought for years. The ministry of Peter Cartwright, Benjamin Abbott, and many other itinerants were filled with experiences that seem to us, in this twentieth century, unique. Men fell to the floor as if dead. Others screamed at the top of their voices. Some trembled with fear. Others stared in awe. Others were seized with peculiar bodily movements, as they were brought to the realization that they were lost sinners. Bring these men who had never had a thought of religion to a realization that they are lost in sin, and living in constant danger of Hell's torment, and they are frightened to their wits' end. Every intensely emotional state has its corresponding bodily resonance, which varies according to the temperament, nervous stability, culture and temporary environment of the individual. But bodily resonance is only the physiological expression of the storm that is going on in the psychic self.

A very widely known illustration of these convulsive movements was the " jerks," so prominent in the great Kentucky revival about the close of the eighteenth century. Settlers had moved with the western tide more rapidly than the missionaries had followed them. Kentucky was very wicked. There had been little or no gospel preaching there. Many had never seen a Bible or heard a preacher. Into this godless country went Rev. James McGready in the year 1796. During the next few years there was a great awakening. Among these illiterate frontiersmen, all kinds of bodily demonstrations accompanied the awakening. The " jerks " was a wagging of the head from side to side, sometimes so rapidly as to distort the features. It seemed contagious. Even skeptics and those opposed to the revival caught the movement. Stephen says it was feared by some more than smallpox.

Even in this late day I have seen some sit with a vague idiotic gaze, others cry with a loud voice, others praying in deep penitence, seem to involve the whole body, until it would twitch and jerk and heave with all sorts of contortions.

There are thousands of people who cannot seem to understand the extreme play of the emotions observed in the evangelical denominations. Now suppose you were out at sea, in perfect health, and content that all was well, and you would land in a few days. Suddenly there is a crash. " All on deck," cries the captain. This order is scarcely obeyed when he cries again, " To the life preservers; every man for himself." There is a sudden realization that the ship is sinking. You are in immediate danger of being lost. You may swim to safety or some other vessel may pick you up, but at the present there is nothing facing you but the briny, icy deep.   Your whole self would be convulsed with fear to its very depths.   Some would scream, others weep, and some of the more nervous would go into hysteria.   Strong men would shudder and weep.   The great Titanic disaster, fresh in the memory of all, is a good example.   Now this is precisely the case with the man who has been living in careless ease when he is brought to a sudden realization that he is lost.   Only the torments of Hell await him at the end of life.   And life, how short!   It may be a year, a day, an hour,— who knows?   He is seized with such consternation and fear that his whole body, his whole self, is involuntarily, but none the less completely, involved.

When the burden is lifted and faith gains attention, and one first realizes that God forgives, the whole self is let loose.   There is such a complete and sudden shifting of the dynamic center of psychic action that then, if ever, the whole emotional self is let loose.   Now if you know the subject, you will know about how to expect him to act when converted.   The quiet, reserved person will be equally complaisant then.   The loud, boisterous person will be demonstrative.   The quick-tempered person will usually be pretty loud.   The sympathetic one will sit down and weep for joy. The contagion so often visible is of a sympathetic character. Tears of joy in one's eyes will evoke them from another. One shouting makes another shout, " Hallelujah."

Now those whose religious training has been in those sects which do not emphasize a deep sense of sin, and hence not so deep a sense of deliverance, cannot understand it. They look at the proceedings of a revival in some evangelical church with as much curiosity as a child looking at a circus, and sometimes with less appreciation and understanding of what is going on. But let such an one continue the illustration of the wrecked vessel as used above. Suppose, just as all hope seemed lost and the horror stricken passengers and crew were about resigned to the fate of a watery grave, as the ship was gradually but surely sinking, another ship appears. She has heard the alarms sent out by wireless, and is heading to the rescue under full steam. Let your fancy paint the picture for a moment. There will be all kinds of expressions of joy, according to the several natures of the individuals. There would be shouts and hurrahs, and tears as well. They would be ready to carry the captain of the rescuing vessel on their shoulders. They would be ready to hug and kiss him. They would be ready to give him liberal perquisites from their means. He saved their lives. Now this just dimly pictures the state of man at conversion. When he realizes that " once I was lost, but now I am saved," there is the same sudden shifting of the mind from an extremely morbid state to one of extreme joy. All the forces of the self will be relaxed and you will find an outlet through the emotions, unless restrained, and with the sudden freeing of the burden, the emotions will bubble over before restraint is thought of. The emotions overflow at the realization that the soul, having satisfied the demands of God, enjoys his approval. When the soul has repented, and through faith is relieved of the burden of sin, it cannot help being happy.

But here comes the Baptist, who believes that the job is not complete until he is immersed. Although happily converted, he is not fully saved until he is immersed. One must be immersed backward, another forward; one once, another three times. As is his faith, so is it unto him. If his emotions were excited at his conversion, they will again be noticed at his baptism. It is no uncommon thing for one with an emotional nature to come up out of the water shouting, or singing, or weeping as the case may be. Why again? From the satisfaction that he has done what he believes God wishes him to do.

We see some get up from prayer shouting,

others at experience meetings or at the communion board, or at the performance of any other marked Christian duty. We, as Christians, have no mortgage on emotional demonstrations upon the observance of religious rites. The old Greeks danced in frenzy before their gods. The Babylonians praised their gods with a loud noise, and with the sound of musical instruments. Those who are familiar with Ben Hur are impressed with the dance before the heathen temple. The American Indians were lost in revelry in their dances before the Great Spirit. Some of the African tribes are exuberant during the course of human sacrifice. Hindoos will rejoice at the hope of Nirvana.

I think I am guilty of no sacrilege when I say that, psychologically, the experience is the same in all these cases. First, there was the contemplated duty, a morbid state of the feeling of human insufficiency, a realization of the necessity of propitiation before the God, real or imaginary. Second, with the performance of the rite the mind is immediately freed from its morbid state. There is the feeling of satisfaction that the soul has done its duty, and God is well pleased. This sudden shifting of the dynamic center of psychosis effects the whole self, involves the whole mind. The more emotional the nature of the subject, the more explosive the force.

There are some communities where they scarcely consider a man religious unless he can shout. And there are some sects that rather urge the full sway of the emotions. I am glad they are few, for experiences born out of pure emotion are as ephemeral as the emotions that gave them birth. The most emotional are not always the most godly. The loudness of the emotions depends on the nature of the man and not on his moral worth. There is always a sort of unification of the self. In emotional natures we find the other traits in sympathy with it. For further study and explanation of all that we have said, let us examine a few cases I have known and studied personally.

Case A. is a man about thirty-five years old. When converted he shouted an hour. Whenever anyone else became demonstrative, he would soon catch it. He was emotional in all things. At a game of ball he could yell himself hoarse for his side. At a flag raising he could throw up his hat and hurrah as loud as anyone in the crowd. He is an extremely high tempered man. He becomes angry in an instant under the least provocation. He is rather self-conceited, although not too capable, being of scant culture and education and devoid of refinement. But he seemed sincere. He seemed to be a good man. He came from a family of shouters. I have seen him shout an hour at different times.

Was he more godly than the others, or did he simply resign all control of himself, and hand his body over to the automatic action of uncontrolled emotion? When I remember that in a fit of temper, because his opinions were not honored, he became the means of dividing his church, I must conclude that it was not more grace that made him shout so, but just a more boisterous nature.

Case B. is a woman of sixty. Her predisposing characteristics are similar to Case A. She also is extremely emotional. She had a habit of patting folks she liked on the cheek or shoulder. When, in an exciting meeting, her emotions were aroused, she would go all over the congregation slapping people on the cheek so hard that it would make their cheeks burn. On asking her about it once, she said she had no knowledge at all of her actions when she was happy. From years of acquaintance with her I have reason to believe she is a good woman,— that is, judging from the fruits as in the other case. Why those boisterous acts of which she seemed to have no knowledge? I should call the conation in this case of the kind that Ladd calls " random-automatic," not being willed at all. When she saw someone converted or heard of a glorious conversion, or contemplated her own deliverance from sin and

God's goodness to her through life, her rejoicing was such that she resigned all self-control, all intellection, for the time, and she was in the automatic control of subconsciousness and reflex action, as was the case with case A.

Case C. was a man about thirty when converted. He was of a highly emotional nature, illiterate and subject to epileptic fits. He was deeply penitent for several days. While earnestly praying at the altar several nights, his whole body as well as his soul seemed involved. I was not well acquainted with him up to this time. Several of the brethren told me to look out for him to have a fit when he was converted. Sure enough. Suddenly he ceased praying for a moment, while I was explaining to him that he must believe God's promise. Then he fell back on the floor in a fit. There he lay prostrate, body twitching slightly, frothing at the mouth, just as when he had a fit at any other time. In about two minutes he revived, and jumping to his feet, shouted the most violently I have ever seen, kicking chairs over and almost creating a panic among the women and children, who feared he would jump on their toes. After a few minutes he fell back on a pew completely exhausted, and began to regain consciousness. But he did not know anything that had happened. His weak nervous system would not stand the sudden shifting of the dynamic center of psychic action.   He always had a fit when under intense excitement.

Case D. was one of those quiet, rather conservative, men.   He was usually slow to think and as slow to act.   He was good-natured, rather jovial, never boisterous, but rather full of fun.   He enjoyed no pleasure more than a visit from some friend.   When under intense conviction I am told he cried like a child. When converted he began scratching his head and laughed until he became hysterical.   I have seen him have many of these laughing spells, when his religious emotions were stirred. He was not unconscious of his actions, as were the former examples.   But the laugh was spontaneous, just as a laugh is unavoidable when one sees or hears a ridiculous thing.   If I would call on him to pray, he would laugh as soon as he began thanking God for his goodness and bounty despite our unworthiness.   Sometimes he would fall into such a paroxysm of laughter, with the tears streaming down his cheeks, that he could not finish the prayer at all.   He was a veteran of the Civil War, and had passed through some trying experiences there, and had had some thrilling experiences since.   While he was relating some of his experiences to me in his home one day, " Oh, how good the Lord has been to me," he said, and immediately the tears rolled down his cheeks unbidden, and his body shook with the characteristic laugh.

Case E. is a woman of the kindhearted, sympathetic type, who has been God-fearing from childhood. She does not remember the day when she did not pray and believe God. She is fairly intelligent, with about an average education. She believes not only in a religion of faith, but of good deeds also. Never a beggar or even a stray dog goes away from her door hungry. She is very quiet and reserved upon all occasions. When in sorrow, although broken up to the very depths of her soul, she says very little about it. It was my very sad lot to bury her mother. Although her sorrow was unutterably deep, and her cheeks wet with tears, you could scarcely hear a sob; but the depths of her whole being were so broken up that she neither ate nor slept. In scenes of religious excitement she acted just as I had expected. She sat down in a corner in quiet meditation without a word or a sob, with just a teardrop trickling down her cheek. Was she a good woman? If we are to judge by the fruits, she was far better than the first examples who were so loud in their profession.

Case F. is a young man who was a great favorite of his mother, and who took his mother into his confidence on all subjects. He was of a quiet, even temperament. His greatest passion seemed to be his devotion for his mother. When he was converted his first thought was, " I must tell my mother." He ran out of the church and across the fields to tell his mother.

Case G. is a laugher. He was one of those men who saw and enjoyed the ridiculous in everything. No man ever enjoyed hearing or telling a joke more than he. I have seen him so amused at the least trifle that his whole body would be convulsed with laughter. He would sometimes fall to the floor and roll and laugh. He is kindhearted, sympathetic, free-hearted and liberal. He would give his last cent to help a needy brother. When he was converted, he laughed until he became hysterical, losing all control of mind and body for the time. The force of the change was so explosive that for the time he knew nothing of his surroundings. His wife was converted in a meeting held by the writer. Much of the paroxysms of laughter experienced at his conversion was repeated. When his emotions were excited by any religious observance, he would laugh until the tears rolled down his cheeks.

It is needless to give further examples. I could give many more, but these will suffice to show the general trend of religious emotion, and prove the two propositions with which we started,— that the emotions are no measure of the piety of the individual either way, and that there is a unity in the mental self that makes the expression of the various emotions harmonize.

There is a contagion about the various expressions of feeling that we cannot ignore. Let one of a crowd of shouters begin, and the others will follow. There is a sympathetic tendency to the human soul. Take a crowd of laughing girls. One may begin to laugh with very little provocation; soon all will be roaring with laughter, and may continue for a whole afternoon. If you see some one laugh, you are apt to smile even before you see or hear anything to laugh at. So, also, if you see some one cry, a teardrop will come in your eye unbidden. This sympathetic nature was a part of the human side (or divine, shall I say?) of our Saviour. When Mary and Martha told him their sorrow, he wept with them.

Now when the intellect is silent, and the body is given over to the automatic action prompted by the impulses and emotions, in any other line physicians call it hysteria. Psychologically we must place much of these demonstrations in the same category. There is a religious hysteria, and we are all subject to it at times,— that is, if there is any concentration of the self on religion. It may come during any religious observance, or even during the quiet meditations of the chamber of prayer.

Prof. James seems to regard these ecstasies and fevers,—" the earthquakes and volcanoes of religious experience," as Peabody calls them, — as normal aspects of religious life, but I cannot altogether agree with him. If this were true, religion would be intermittent and spasmodic, not stable. But religion is a LIFE. And life must be continuous. As soon as life ceases, it is not life but death. It is true that the stream of conscious life will show ripples and billows sometimes. But these are pathological rather than normal experiences. I am not prone to attach too much importance to them as separate events, but would rather consider them mere incidents in the development of religion. Prof. Peabody says: " These abnormal incidents, these volcanic eruptions, in fact, make more impressive the orderliness and continuity which mark the normal condition of religious life."

It is argued by some that an occasional stir in the emotions strengthens the religious life, starts it off with renewed vigor. But this is not always true. At the expiration of an intensely emotional season, whether of joy or sorrow, the intellect is usually extremely sluggish. Any emotion, unless killed by its opposite, must gradually wear itself out. In the " dull state of nerves " following, any obsession for evil has a peculiarly good chance to gain hypertrophy of the attention.

It is possible to force an emotional state through what is usually the outward means of its expression. But when the emotion is thus forced, there is usually less contagion among the crowd. I once had a member in my congregation who would repeatedly try to force a shout. She would go through the motion until she would summon the mental state at least partially. A negro of the less intelligent type can clap his hands and sing until he works himself up into a perfect frenzy of religious emotion.

I remember one company I found in one of the smaller denominations, who actually tried to make a penitent shout before she was converted. Several were standing around her clapping their hands and shouting, trying their best to make her shout, thinking that with the emotion might come the experience. But it cannot be so. Such methods are enough to disgust any intelligent worker.

While the intelligent expression of religious joy is always refreshing to all around, the emotions ought not to be allowed to gain control to the suppression of reason and intelligence. I think we play on the emotions too much sometimes. We ought not to aim at the excitation of the feelings.   There are thousands brought into the church while the feelings are excited, and reason and intelligence not active, whose religion is as ephemeral as the emotion that gave it birth.   To appeal to the feelings is to appeal to the very lowest part of the mind. Why, the brutes have all the emotions.   Let all appeals of a moral nature be to the intelligence and reasoning, to the better judgment.   When a man, after deliberately reasoning over the matter, decides to serve God, he does not usually go back.   But with the one who is brought into the church by a wave of excitement of the emotions, his experience has no foundation in the mental self when the emotion has subsided.

CHAPTER VIII

CONSCIENCE

Conscience is no separate faculty, however much theologians may tell us about an inner voice. It is judgment, combining feeling and intellection in the approbation of good and the condemnation of evil. And this is clearly influenced by birth, education and environment, especially education. Some one defined conscience as: "My opinion of myself according to the best light I possess." This would not satisfy the theological student. For his benefit I might revise the above a little. It is God's opinion of myself and actions as revealed to me through my intelligence, or as revealed to me through my own self or soul. But it can only be revealed to me through terms I already understand, which makes it depend entirely upon my education, and that as influenced by both birth and environment. As we proceed to examine each of these facts separately, we shall better understand why people who are equally conscientious differ so widely in their opinions as to many lines of conduct.

Do we inherit some of the opinions of our forefathers? I think it would be nearer right to say that we inherit their tendencies, impulses, appetites, etcetera, and that opens up the way for us to agree with them in judgment. The influence of birth is due more to the fact that the circumstances and environment of birth determine much of the early education. A child born in a wicked home will have little moral training and little moral sense unless in later years he comes in contact with better moral environment. On the other hand, the child born in a Christian home, receiving careful moral training from the beginning, will show its effects through life, although brought in contact with evil society afterwards, which may remove some of the polish.

Solomon said, " Train up a child in the way he should go, and when he is old he will not depart from it." The Roman Catholic church claims that if a child is carefully trained until seven years old, he will always be a Catholic. Of course there are exceptions to all these rules. But all must admit that the young mind is far more susceptible to moral impressions, and impressions of youth are far more permanent than those of after years.

It is a sad fact that in many Christian homes the child does not receive careful training. The children of the present and last generation have received far better training in all other things than in religion. Business and pleasure are the two chief concerns of the age. Many parents express far more satisfaction at the development of keen business ideas than of acute moral sense in the child. There is a laxity in the discipline of children, the fruits of which are already evident. Let the child enjoy its youth. Let it sow its wild oats. Do not curb them down too closely. This seems to be the fashionable attitude of the day on the subject. In many homes moral questions are seldom discussed at all, and the only religious training the child receives is an occasional hour at Sunday School. Thrice fortunate is the child in a home where there will be real Christian example and training. Conscience, to be a safe guard and guide, must have for its foundation a correct moral education. Wrong opinions will surely be the basis of wrong decisions.

In view of these facts, let us look a little further into education as the foundation principle of conscience. For an example,— there was a time when a certain man on the farm saw no impropriety in taking a glass of hard cider. He thought that the harm in drinking was in getting drunk, and not in an occasional drink of some light beverage. He never thought of taking a drink of whiskey or beer. He never took a drink of anything intoxicating in a bar or other public place.   He was taught that this was wrong.   But his father put away a barrel of cider every fall.   The father drank of it and so did the son.   Neither ever drank anything strong at any other time or place.   I know them both and respect them as gentlemen of Christian integrity.   The son drank the cider without any consciousness of wrong, although he would not even take that away from home, except among intimate friends.   But as he grew older and saw more of the world, he saw some ruined by drink who had started on cider.   He saw the wrong of it, and determined to leave it alone, not only for his own safety, but for the sake of his example.

In my younger days, I used to play checkers and dominoes occasionally.   I considered it an innocent bit of amusement.   But I have not played a game of either for fifteen years.   Thousands spend their evenings at such diversions, but to me it would be a sinful waste of time.   I could give other instances to show the change of conscience during my own life, as well as the influence of early education, and of later observation and experience.

A man's environment also influences his education, and hence his judgment.   His environment may be such as to prevent what good instruction is available from gaining attention.

A man's surroundings do absorb much of his attention, and they may be such as to hinder any deep moral impressions or reflections. Some things may be done repeatedly without any condemnation of conscience, but after mature reflection, which means but the concentration of the attention upon the subject, we may decide that it was wrong. After this decision of our better judgment, we will feel condemned if we do not obey it. Again, environment may be so wicked as to immediately counteract any impression for good by usurping the attention before there is time for reflection.

There can be no set rules of conscience, because all are not educated alike. The Hindu mother will cast her babe in the Ganges for conscience's sake. But our American mothers would refrain from such action for conscience's sake. There have been various heathen tribes who practised human sacrifice in their ignorance for conscience's sake. But surely all civilized peoples would refrain for conscience's sake. Catholics adore the saints for conscience's sake, but Protestants refrain from all such observance for conscience's sake. A man's conscience will never condemn him for what his intellect says is right, however wrong his judgment.

From what has been said (and examples could be continued *ad infinitum*) it is evident that conscience, or rather the foundation of conscience, is a system of judgments as to the rightness or wrongness of acts. Where there has been no reflection upon an act, and hence no judgment upon its moral quality, conscience will be silent. These judgments will not only be determined by intellectual decision, but will be colored by our sentiments and strengthened by our emotions. Now judgment in any line may change from first opinions, after mature deliberation, weighing carefully the evidences and consequences on both sides. For example, the early Christians, being of Jewish descent, insisted upon the circumcision of the gentile converts; but after mature deliberation of the elders it was decided an unnecessary and useless burden. The Greeks ate the meat offered to idols, but after conversion they were taught to abstain from it.

After an intelligent conception of right and wrong, there must be a focusing of the attention upon the act and a comparison of the act with these judgments previously formed. If the deed has been at variance with the set habits of life, there will be little difficulty in focusing the attention upon it. Indeed, it will steal into our attention unbidden, because it is rebellious against the habitual center of interest and also against our other acts in the same line still lingering in subconsciousness. But if the habits of life are not in accordance with the best judgment of the subject, the habitual center of interest is not controlled by reason and common sense at all, but by the lower impulses of the body. The more confirmed one is in the habit of acting against his better judgment, the less such action will attract attention. And unless it does gain attention, he will feel no condemning conscience, for there will be no introspection at the time. But a little introspection, a little examination of our behaviour in the light of our best judgment, may awaken the disapproval of conscience afterward. In this very way one may go on in sin many years after it has become a set habit, without giving it any attention, and without any reproof from conscience, until some obsession from without directs attention to the act. Then, after a little introspection, conscience may suddenly arise with dynamic force. But what is the voice we hear? Is it the voice of God, or is it the voice of our own soul? Is it not the realization of sin by our own soul? We realize the disapproval of God because it is our intelligent judgment that we have disobeyed him. Until we formed this judgment, we heard no voice of disapproval.

Peter smote Malchus, cutting off his ear in

defence of his Lord.   He thought he was right.
But Jesus rebuked him.   He acted according
to his best judgment.   But should he have repeated the act after the Master's rebuke, conscience would have condemned him, because his
judgment was changed.   Paul conscientiously
persecuted the Christians.   He was a strict
Jew and believed with his whole heart that
Christ was an impostor, and that his disciples
were disseminating a false and injurious doc-
trine.   But after his conversion he preached
this same Christ with more zeal than any of
them, and was willing to die for the gospel's
sake, because he now judged it to be right.
Martin Luther in his younger life was a staunch
Catholic and a devout monk, but after years
of study and reflection upon God's word, he became the chief agitator and instigator of the
Reformation.

If, as Peabody has it, " religion is education,
and education is religion," surely there is no
department of religion so dependent upon education as conscience.   Conscience is by no
means an infallible guide.   Persons under illusions or of erroneous judgment may form all
sorts of peculiar judgments, and conscientiously carry them out.   Of course, before God
we are not responsible for erroneous judgments, honestly formed.   If we obey our best
judgment, we will not fall into voluntary sin,

so that while conscience is not infallible, it is a fairly safe guide, providing we are always open to conviction and instruction, not prejudicing our minds against further acquirement of truth.

CHAPTER IX

ILLUSIONS AND HALLUCINATIONS

The very title of this chapter would be an offence to many good people. All psychologists agree, however, that illusions and hallucinations are part of the waking experience of us all. This is true in religion as well as in practical life. Continued focusing of the attention not only intensifies sensations, but actually creates them sometimes. This is the strength of hypnotism and Christian Science.

Now an illusion is a misconception or misinterpretation of something that really exists, but is misunderstood. It may be due to defective sense perception or to erroneous interpretation of what is perceived. An hallucination is purely imaginary and altogether subjective.

These abnormal experiences in connection with religion may begin with the first realization of the moral sense, or with the first awakening. The deeper and more dynamic this awakening, the more the subject is apt to suffer from illusions and hallucinations. The case of

Benjamin Abbott, already referred to, is a good illustration. He was haunted by the most terrible dreams, and would awake, thinking them true. When he rode home in the wagon, thinking the Devil was right after him, it was as real to him as if true. When a person is in this morbid state, the least bodily disorder is greatly exaggerated, because the attention has been focused upon sin and death. With the least disorder, the subject thinks he will surely die. A good example is the man who dreamed he was to die at sunrise, while he was under deep conviction. When he awoke, he summoned his doctor and paid him well to stay with him until after that hour, although the physician found every organ working normally and well. The morbid state of deep conviction had continued in subconsciousness while the active self was asleep. (This accounts for many of our dreams.) His waking thoughts were troubled because of sin and of possible death unsaved. Subconsciousness had only continued this strain while he slept.

Many also see these false experiences at conversion. One sees a great light before him. Another hears strange voices and peculiarly sweet music. Another says that upon opening his eyes everything looks so bright. We hear it often said that all nature seems more beautiful. Some have even thought they saw the Saviour with outstretched arms extending his mercy to them. Most of these experiences can be explained by the sudden shifting of the mind from an extremely morbid state to an extremely happy state, as the soul believes that he is saved by faith. Things look better when interpreted by a joyful mind than when interpreted by a mind that is crushed by the burden of sin, just as much as they differ in appearance in the light of the sun and in the darkness of midnight. In the last case mentioned there was complete hallucination, due possibly to complete coneentration of the attention upon the mercy of Jesus, coupled with the imagined picture of his person,— possibly some picture of him the subject had seen,— lingering in memory.

The boldest imposition upon those who are subject to illusions, especially when there is extreme hypertrophy of attention, is Christian Science. Psychologically, I can see little difference between this and other forms of hypnotism, except that the subject is kept under the spell longer. First of all, there is a wrong education. The subject is deluded into a belief that all pain is subjective and not objective, and that it is sin to use outward means for its relief, notwithstanding the fact that both Old and New Testaments mention examples where God directed the use of outward remedies. The prophet of God directed Hezekiah to put a fig poultice on his boils, and they were healed. Fig poultice is yet considered a very good remedy to bring boils to a head. Christ made a clay poultice and put it on the blind man's eyes.

Upon this erroneous teaching as a foundation, the attention is controlled so as to keep it off any bodily disorders, and directed in the channel of the will to be well. As I said in the beginning, repeated attention not only intensifies sensations but creates new ones. If you do not think so, try it. Close your eyes and fancy you see some form before you. Keep your mind strictly upon that. Completely focus your attention upon it, and after a while you will actually imagine you see the object before you. Here is a good illustration: You are waiting for a carriage; every little noise will sound like its approach, and you will imagine you hear it even when there is no noise. This is much of the secret of faith healing. You must have faith in it. Your faith in it is then made the means of concentrating your attention upon a speedy and permanent cure. This complete hypertrophy of attention strengthens faith until it surmounts all obstacles, even existing bodily conditions. Then tell the patient he will notice rapid improvement, each day being a little better. Or tell him that on a certain day he will notice a great change for the better. The faith is so strong, and the attention so completely focused, as to produce the sensation of improvement, although the body may be weaker and the disease actually worse. Patients have steadfastly professed to be better until death.

There are cases of hysteria, hypochondria and other nervous diseases, where much of the trouble is illusory, that this method does cure by dispelling the illusion of the patient. But thousands are thus deluded into neglect of bodily conditions until disease reaches an incurable stage. I have known parents to allow children to sicken and die because they thought it wrong to call a doctor.

We are inclined to place spiritualism in the same category. The medium or spiritualist, by vivid concentration of her attention, imagines she sees and talks with the souls of the departed. Peculiarly, they usually say what she either wishes or expects them to say. They can only delude those who have perfect faith in them, for unless there is perfect confidence, they will not be able to control the attention sufficiently to delude them. This is only another form of the abuse of extreme hypertrophy of attention.

Another illusion to which the superstitious mind is subject is the misinterpretation of every little noise about the place. The negroes and other illiterate races, and the more ignorant of our own race, are peculiarly susceptible to these illusions.   They believe in " tokens " as a direct communication from God.   I know a woman who used to come to my father's house during my childhood, who believes greatly in tokens of all kinds.   If a door cracks, as they will, especially in a new house, she immediately says that some one in the family will be sick or die very soon.   She is a conscientious Christian, but as ignorant as you find.

If there is severe illness in the house, it is easy for such superstitious folks to interpret any little thing as a token.   A neighbor of mine told me not many days ago about a token he heard in a death chamber in which he had been sitting.   Everything was perfectly quiet.   The patient seemed gradually weakening.   All at once the door opened.   Of course that was a token, and in a couple of hours the patient died.   The door may not have been well latched.   Had there been no one sick in the house, he would not have noticed it.   The secret of the whole thing was his already focused attention on the expected death of his friend.

An old darkey who lived on a corner of my father's farm during my boyhood died from heart disease.   As the end was approaching, another old darkey, who was helping to care for him, saw something like a white pigeon flit by the door. It may have been one, but when he went to the door it was gone. Of course it was a token.

In another case there was a rap at the front door. The lady, on going to the door, found no one there. Shortly after coming back to the sick room the patient died. Of course this' was a token. The door may have cracked as they often do. It may have been the wind, a dog, or any one of many things. I wonder if this lady never answered a supposed knock at the door and found no one there before.

A certain very godly woman whom I knew was paralyzed, and was dying. When the doctor came in the morning, he said that her pulse indicated death in a very few hours. Her two daughters were sitting quietly by her bedside awaiting the end. Her eyes were set and the pulse almost ceased. Their minds were completely centered upon the death of this good woman, their mother. Suddenly they heard a rustling like that of silk. Of course this was the angels coming for the soul of their mother. Whether they heard anything I cannot say. They may have heard some little noise they misunderstood. But have you never fancied you heard peculiar sounds when the attention was so completely fixed that active consciousness was silent? How about the ringing and singing in

the ears just as we are about to lose consciousness in sleep, or even when day-dreaming.

I think the proper explanation for the whole
thing would be, first the complete focusing of
the attention upon the expected death of the
patient, and either an illusory interpretation
by the superstitious mind of some little thing
that happens, or else an entire hallucination.
All these illusions come only to those who believe
in them. In many cases it is complete hallucination. In others it is the misinterpretation
of some little event by a superstitious mind that
is rendered morbid by the terrible suspense, for
they are seldom, if ever, discernible to disinter-
ested, intelligent observation.

There is yet another class of hallucinations
which come when the conscious self is not in possession and the person is controlled by subconsciousness. They are much like dreams, but
frequently more vivid. We refer now to the
supposed appearances of the departed ones
when the active consciousness is morbid or in-
active during sickness, or in a trance, which is
nothing more, psychologically, than a prolonged sleep-dream.

Let us cite a few cases. Several years ago a
patient was suffering severely from inflamma-
tory rheumatism, delirious much of the time.
One day, while in this semi-delirious condition,

she aroused from the stupor and said to her nurse, " I have had such a pleasant experience; my mother came and stood by my side and communed with me." She says to this day that she saw her mother as plainly as she ever did while she was alive. The father of this woman claimed to see his departed wife several times during his last illness, and would talk to her as though she were in the room.

Another woman whom I knew claimed to see her mother and her aunt in her last hours, and seemed amazed that those around could not see them as well, it seemed so vivid to her.

Now in all of these cases, and in thousands of others of this kind, the active consciousness is dormant because of sickness, and the organism is controlled by subconsciousness. There is also a trace of belief in spiritualism, else when the subject awakes they would not accredit it as true, but consider it a dream or hallucination. What actually happens is a vivid appearance of a memory image of the departed one, which is all the more vivid because it has complete possession of the mind, active consciousness being dormant, as in a dream. When the patient arouses from the stupor or delirium, it seems real to him.

Kindred to these are the expressions of many souls as they leave the body for the beyond. Do they catch a glimpse of the beyond, or are their experiences hallucinations, caused by fancy picturing that which they expect the beyond to be? It may be both. I would not say that it is impossible for the soul, just as it lays down the body, to catch a glimpse of the beyond. I think, however, it may be explained psychologically. First, there is a fancied picture of the future, which has been present for years and has grown more vivid as it approached. The saved soul knows he is saved. And faith has all along pictured the city of gold with Christ and his angels. Thus Moody said that he saw earth receding, heaven opening, and heard God calling him. Another said, " I am sweeping through the gates clothed in his image." Some have visions of angels. Others hear peculiarly sweet music. Still others see the spirits of departed friends. Some have professed to see the Saviour seated upon a throne.

The sinner knows he is lost. He has been taught a burning Hell filled with demons and lost souls. Hence he goes out of the world with the most horrible visions. One went out crying at the top of his voice, " Fire, fire, fire! Oh, I see fire! " Some have visions of demons and hear the cries of lost souls, etcetera. The consciousness of sin and that the last chance for repentance is past but adds to the horror of his last moments.

There is this fact to favor the psychological explanation of these experiences. They usually agree with the preconceived idea of the future. He who expects glory has a vision of glory. He who knows he is damned has a vision of Hell. He who does not believe anything has no vision at all; it is just a leap into the dark. Those who believe in and expect a future life will see it just as they expect it. I think, after all, it is a vision of faith. But it surely shows to those around, how beautiful is the death of the faithful.

CPSIA information can be obtained
at www.ICGtesting.com
Printed in the USA
BVHW051542040319
541706BV00022B/1338/P